Letters From The L

AFORI PUBLISHING

First Edition 2016

Translations
Catherine Yekimov, Inge R, Lizze Vrijsen

Special thanks to Yad Vashem Archive for there help

© The content of the letters are the property of Yad Vashem. Unauthorized use and/or duplication of this material without express and written permission from Yad Vashem is strictly prohibited.

This book was written in the memory of the Ledermann family

Table of contents

1. INTRODUCTION

2. AMSTERDAM

3. ELLEN CITROEN DEPORTATION TO WESTERBORK

4. ILSE FRANZ AND SANNE DEPORTATION TO WESTERBORK

5. THE LEDERMANN FAMILY AFTER THE WAR

6. REFERENCES

Family Tree

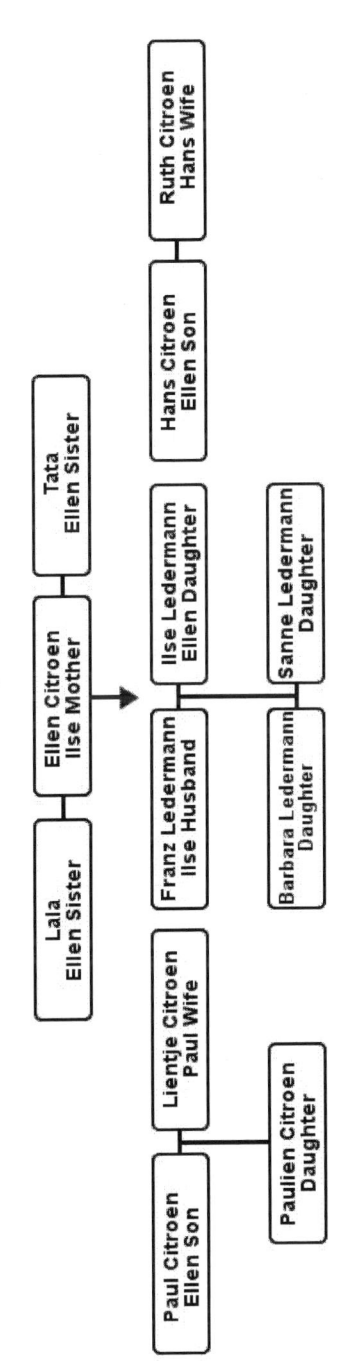

- **Lala** — Ellen Sister
- **Ellen Citroen** — Ilse Mother
- **Tata** — Ellen Sister

- **Paul Citroen** — Ellen Son
  - **Lientje Citroen** — Paul Wife
  - **Paulien Citroen** — Daughter

- **Ilse Ledermann** — Ellen Daughter
  - **Franz Ledermann** — Ilse Husband
  - **Barbara Ledermann** — Daughter
  - **Sanne Ledermann** — Daughter

- **Hans Citroen** — Ellen Son
  - **Ruth Citroen** — Hans Wife

Introduction

The Ledermanns were a Jewish family living in Berlin, Germany. The rise of the Nazis in 1933 led the family to migrate to the Netherlands as did many other Jewish families at that time. They rented an apartment on 37th Noorder Amstellaan St. which is now renamed to Churchill-laan St. in Amsterdam, tens of meters from Merwedeplein square where the Frank family lived. The girls: Barbara, born 1925, was registered to Jeker School on 84th Jekerstraat St. in the class of Margot Frank. The younger sister Sanne, born 1928, registered to the Montessori School on 43rd Niersstraat St. in the class of Anne Frank and Hanneli Goslar. The head of the family, Franz Ledermann, worked along with Hanneli Goslar's father, Hans Goslar, in an office opened by him for Jewish refugee aid. Life returned to normal until the German invasion to the Netherlands on May 10th, 1940. Gradually the lives of the Jews began being increasingly restricted with each day.

The first letter in this book dated July 3rd, 1942 was written mere days before Margot Frank received her call up letter on July 5th. This letter led to the immediate entry of the Frank family into hiding the next day, on July 6th. At this stage, the large hysteria has already begun when hundreds of call up letters for the supposedly "work in the service of Germany" were sent to many young people.

Families tried different methods in dealing with the decrees, starting from receiving working permits in the service of the Reich, which could postpone these so-called call up letters, and obtaining falsified certificates which did not have the big J stamp that marked the Jews as did the Ledermanns, entry into hiding as did the Franks and various other methods to avoid deportation.

Franz Ledermann's good connections at the Judenrat allowed him to postpone and delay the deportation of the family for about a year, but eventually the Ledermanns Ilse, Franz and Sanne were deported in the same Razzia in which the Goslars were deported. The family stayed in Westerbork transit camp for 5 months, from June 20th to November 16th, on which they were sent to Auschwitz and murdered on the day of their arrival, on November 19th, 1943. Ellen, the mother of Ilse and grandmother of Sanne, was sent to Bergen Belsen and died on January 6th, 1945 from exhaustion, starvation and diseases. Barbara survived the war hiding with falsified certificates and migrated to America after the war.

This book contains 51 letters that were written by the family members in the period of July 1942 to November 1943, and is the Ledermanns diary of letters that describes the family's struggle with the impossible living conditions at the time.

The letters in this book were mostly written in German by most of the family members, excluding the girls who wrote in Dutch. In the letters, the family members used many different nicknames. Sanne, which is the nickname given to her by Anne Frank in her diary, is named in the letters as: Suzzana, Zanna, Susie, Sannchen, Suusje, Susje. To avoid confusion that these are different people and due to the many names that appear in the letters, I changed the names of the family members to fixed names throughout the book. The only exception I made is with the letters sent to Barbara from Westerbork the family members use the name Lottie and Lizze Not to reveal her identity, so I kept it in the translation.

My remarks appear at the bottom of the pages to clarify different subjects in the letters. Remarks that appear inside the letters are remarks that were added to the letters by the family members themselves or by the person who transcribed the letters, seemingly Tamar Shoshan, formerly known as Dolly Citroen, a family member of the mother's side, who passed the letters to the Yad Vashem museum.

Amsterdam

3. 7.42

Paul and Lientje, My dear,

The situation is rather difficult for you these days and you have no idea how since last night, Franz has been seriously debating your problem and does not actually know what to advice on the subject.. Everything can work out, but it can also worsen.

He is considering, examining, committing, rejecting, and as a matter of fact, he is completely hopeless.

And he said that, in fact, we cannot advise our closest people, since we are too involved with them.

Today, old Mrs. Pan Hovan eventually passed away, gladly it did not happen on Mom's birthday.

The kids asked Mom to allow the funeral to start from the house on Hondecoeter st. so the body could remain in the house until Tuesday.

Licenses are not given for riding the tramcar as a matter of principle. It would have been better if you came here otherwise Paul would be completely stuck. Franz is going to the Y. R (Judenrat) by bicycle now which is too tiring for him. He hopes to succeed and return to a state in which he can work at home. Keep well. I am crossing my fingers. Yours, Ilse.

Sanne received an 8 in German, 7 in everything else.

3. 7. 42

Dear Paul,

Although I have not completely lost hope for surprises I must admit to you that at the moment, the situation seems in a way that can be described as fixed... which is also an understatement. In these situations I being preached by the family, by whom emotions of dismay consume the will to endure the hardships and do not help better the situation.

I really think that we are getting closer to a situation where we can endure what is happening by standing tall. However, had we not been rather spoiled? Had there not always been groups of people who suffered and were chased after? And is it not injustice to completely spend the years of our lives which will be considered for us in the final reckoning? And are there not millions of people out there whose fate is thousands of times worse than ours? I suggest despising the dangers that threaten us! It is a mistake to assume that the depressors are the happy, and that the depressed are the miserable! "In days of hardship, keep your spirits good" (In Latin, in the original letter), claimed Horatius, who was experienced in hardships. Let's attempt to stay optimistic?

Let's closely examine the dangers. For the both of us, You and I, there is no, as this stage, immediate danger to be sent to labor camps in Germany with our families, since for now the limit is until age 40 solely, if so, the tooth brush should not be packed yet. The investigation regarding Lientje second grandfathers is of course unpleasant. In a scenario in which the investigation ends in a negative way, something I hope will not happen, the woman and Hilda will be recognized as belonging to our race. That as well is not that terrible, we will need to get used to it and if all of you will have to move to Amsterdam, we will at least have the opportunity to meet more often at times.

A hard question is, how we should treat Paulien not signing up in advance. I heard that now there isn't a necessity to carry the registration permit along with the identity certificate, I thought that there is no need to sign her up but in light of your message regarding the investigation of the information regarding the second grandfather, I am afraid that the question regarding Paulien registration will come up, and hence, my opinion is that, now, perhaps, we should apologize and sign her up late. It is very hard to estimate where these investigations could lead. On the other hand, maybe it is possible to sign her up after the end of the investigation and avoid doing so "voluntarily". I also think that the organization of the whole situation should not be overestimated. Except that, I think that if I was in your position, I would perform the late registration to set free of the uncertainty. Maybe you should try speaking again with the man at the municipality that showed good will, and ask him if he already had a similar case and what were the results of late registration? Maybe it is in his ability to show interest with colleagues at Hague. Try to find something in this direction. At the moment, I think that the man will probably not be able to answer such a question, but better try, it might help seeing with more clarity.

Loving regards to all of you, Yours, Franz.

9th of July, 42

Dear Paul and Lientje,

It was very nice of you to call. It must sound a lot worse from there, although everything is pretty bad. So: 1. everyone who is from the Jewish Council (The following Y.R.) are fully protected for now and so are their families. Before I knew this I was crazily worried for Barbara. All of her friends had received the draft notice. It started on Sunday afternoon. The police handed out the notices from house to house, by which they should appear the next day at 8 and 9 in the morning at the Gestapo.

Included are all men aged 15 to 40, In case of being married then with the families; all single women up to age 40 and all young women from age 16, but there are many 15 year old girls among them. At the Gestapo, they had received a note by which they need to appear on July 15th at 02:30 in the morning at the train station equipped with 2 wool blankets, 2 sheets and food for 3 days, but only items attained by the official distribution, and a suitcase or a backpack with a limited number of items, taken from a detailed list. This operation is called "Transfer for Work in Germany". At first you arrive to a camp in *Drenthe for a medical inspection, afterwards seemingly to East Germany or Czech for work. News had arrived from

Poland that people are being sent to work in Germany. A postcard had arrived from Upper *Silesia from Jews who were sent earlier to Poland, who say that they are working hard, that there are some benefits and that it is tolerable. Here it is promised that mail, packages and money can be sent. The onslaught on the Y.R. is indescribable and there is no chance to receive another job. We tried, vainly, to somehow classify Barbara. Last night, I even asked Clary's father for her hand. But the old Italian was too confused to accept. At the moment, The Y.R. are calling to let us know that today they received an official announcement, by which the young daughters of the Y.R employees are also protected. We do not deserve such joy! There is nothing but tragedies around us.

A lot of families are becoming child-absent. Young and happy couples must leave. Bridget seems the worst to me. Eva Bosa told me that she passed your photographs to Zuid Von Fauzan. Amstel 51 was tall and brave. The few that are like her suffer the least. But the separation from the young children is unbearable. Embraces to you, Yours, Ilse.

• Drenthe is a province of the Netherlands, located in the northeast of the country.

• Silesia is a region of Central Europe now located mostly in Poland, with small parts in the Czech Republic.

July 10th, 42

Dear Paul and Lientje, the continued report for your information:

Starting today it is the turn of the Dutch, everyday 800 to 1,200 people are being loaded. Anyone who is between the ages of 16 and 40 is sent to work in Germany. Ages 40 to 55 are chosen to work in the Netherlands and receive special treatment. All young people must appear at the Gestapo where they will fill a form in case they get "caught". At that time they get a note saying on which train they must board on the way to Westerbork, the camp in the area of Drenthe where the medical examinations take place. The Y.R. helps them fill out the forms which are pretty simple. When regarding married men under the age of 40, the family joins automatically. Divorced women and their children can stay. Regarding release, the orders are as following: people whose work for the community is mandatory, are for now removed from the lists along with people working at the Y.T. and those who work in units affiliated with the Y.R, the School's Union and the Jewish community. Some of the doctors and pharmacists were force to go as well.

Today the phone lines were cut off without notice for a whole group of Jews. Although they were sent messages about ending contracts at August 1st or September 1st, it was seemingly done as a joke. And so on and on. Today I was at Bridget's, who shows exemplary behavior as everyone does really. Friendship will benefit everyone. In any case, we made sure to immunize Barbara against Cholera and

Typhoid. She has to receive 3 shots one of which she already did.

Embraces, Yours, Ilse.

August 22nd, 42

Paulien, my dear!

Oh, how lovely this photograph is, I am very happy and endlessly look at it and only hope I can enjoy it for much longer here at the apartment. Everyone is very excited about it.

It was good to speak with Lientje again, we are made aware again of how things are with one another. I really wanted to write to you after our shock, but it did not work. Composure is the most important thing.

Sanne is finding it hard to imagine going to school and studying again. She has been through a lot and is sensing the existential insecurity very hard these days… It is great that you are living there outside, it helps a lot. I am certain that Lientje had told about the campers.

Tata, again and again, forgot who had given her what, it is good that that mistake cannot be made with your photograph.

If so, Paulien, thank you for the surprise of this pretty gift and thousands of blessings to you, Lientje and

Paul, Yours, Ilse.

September 42

Beloved Children! What a unnecessary statement; Are not children always loved?

And so, I will not be able to bear a cruel fate hurting one of some of them. Myself, I had life full of suffering and happiness, the latter mainly through my four children and their families, all of whom were as close to me as if I had given birth to them myself. And so, I had a rich life. You may not even know just how grateful I am for that to you, but as well to the power I believe in, although I do not know how to call it. I cannot make sure that I will be the one who will be happy her entire life. My only prayer is that none of you will be hurt, rather only me. I will not complain about it under the condition that you will not suffer and will be able to enjoy and see how all the beauty you had seeded blossoms. Do not worry about me! I am very happy about Lientje's visit and only hope we will be here until then. Last night at 8:30, 3 men had come here. They came for Mr. De-Paris and asked me if he lives here and if he is sick. He is lying here, having a heart condition, and his sister is taking care of him. They walked in his room, saw him, and one of them said: "Yes, I can see he has a heart condition", asked to see his medical permit and his sister's Y.R. permit, said "It is okay, good night" and disappeared. I was not worried for even a second.

Lientje, I am asking if it is not too difficult, I would love some carrots, if they are attainable. But only if it is not complicated and they are not too heavy. Of course I will be happy with anything. Maybe a package of flour? I had just baked a cake for Lena. She came to visit me with yesterday up until 11:30 in the evening, it was very pleasant! They also very much enjoyed the beautiful day they had spent at your place. I would really like to spend another day such as that! They also told me, in answer to my questions, that Paulien demands so much of herself, and that she is never pleased with the achievements. I hope that she will soon understand that even without that she is one of the best and that no one has such good grades at elementary school anymore.

Please give her a warm embrace from Grandma even if it doesn't help against her serious ambitions. I will see you on Saturday, Kisses, Mom.

Greetings from Lala and Tata.

September 11th, 42

Dear Paul and Lientje, thank you for all your efforts. Galinka was here, but with Pete we could have found out more. At the moment, there are "gathering actions" here almost every evening.. Almost, towards the holidays they say that there will be a stop. A gentleman-like agreement! Mainly Dutch and many of them are so old. They came to take Bernard and Palo on the evening of the day before yesterday, I do not know if they will be released again. It was the turn of S... they allowed Betsy to stay in bed due to her illness.

The wife of his son and their child were forced to leave but were released again that night because Kurt had just received a certificate saying that he works for a German fur-clothing manufacturer who is employed by the Wehrmacht, and hence is on the list of the Wehrmacht. Such fortune! Besides that, I am not aware of anyone else from ours. Croneheim was ok last night and the Y.R. is helping. The most exciting part is that a letter arrived from Hans and Ruth that I would really like to show mom before I send it to you.

23.9.42

Dear Paul and Lientje, thank you for your letter. The situation with Weininger's wife is extraordinary.

Anyone who had converted to Christianity received such a notification, afterwards they had to come here and receive the stamping. Here they were listed in printed lists. It is pretty strange that in *Scheveningen, nothing is known about this. They say that mixed marriages will receive the same stamping. It says: "The carrier of this certificate is released at this time from working service".

Franz appeared yesterday for classification. He as well is "released at this time", meaning, released due to his certificate. In some time he will receive another invitation, and then will have to obtain a permit from a heart specialist. In addition, he is released due to his work in the Y.R. .

Everything is of course temporary. The day they had arrested Mrs. V, there was huge manhunt for foreign citizens here. They visited Willheimoss again, who was not home at the time but went and sorted himself a stamping at the S.S. the next day because, how surprisingly, he had apparently converted to Christianity as well. And he had the nerve to take Lizzie's identification certificate with him, and ask to have it stamped for her. The first refused to that , but the second said "After all, we do this in family form" and gave him a stamping for Lizzie, as well. Crazy luck! At Hugh's, as well, everyone is still home. They visited them the following evening when everyone was home, and all ended well with the help of a certificate from the Italian consul who was prepared for this. At the same time they had found one Italian man who had a fascist lapel decoration on the flap of his shirt, and with him she spoke Italian. That helped a lot as well. It seems that Fleur and Bernard were already sent to Germany. Hard to describe! ...

I do not believe that we will have peace starting October 1st, even if the shipments to Germany will stop, I assume that in that case they will place us in camps here in the Netherlands, camps that will be formed for this purpose. But to me it seems preferable over Poland. Last night, at 1:00 at night, our doorbell rang. We were scared to death. Though it was one very "cultural" ring that did not repeat itself. I heard a knock on the door. After a while I came down and found a urgent letter for Franz from some woman. Something as this should be banned!

 Embraces, Yours, Ilse

• Scheveningen - districts in Hague

October 3rd, 42

Paulien, my dear,

I was just about to continue reporting to you when your letter arrived. It is lovely when you reply so fast.

It seems to me that the W.M. (Wehrmacht) people have too much interest in your little house and that worries me. Maybe they would like to live in it?

I have good news: first of all, mom and Barbara received an invitation to receive the stamping. Barbara had first received an invitation for the 13th, but today a letter arrived that invites her to receive it tomorrow. These apply to us even on Sunday. Besides that, today I heard about a same case as yours, meaning, forgetting signing up the child and that with no problem receiving the yellow ticket from the station for population registration, even after the stated date. In addition to those, it was made known yesterday that the certificate for the appointment towards registration of mixed marriages as itself can be used as defense in time of gathering from the houses. Because yesterday, after I wrote to you, a lot has happened. First of all, Franz came from the Y.R. with news published by the general secretary Bollela stating that you should be ready and packed in preparation for a giant operation planned for that evening. Five trains stood waiting, meaning, a predicted gathering of 5,000 Jews and a huge number of agents were summoned for the execution of the gathering. The expositor were sent home as early as 5:00, a sign that this time everything will be done without the Y.R. In the worst manner. Solely the stamping, or the invitation for a stamping could help. At 6:00, our friend from the expo Hybol, came full of panic and we were very distraught because B. (Barbara) did not have an invitation for a stamping still. With great excitement we considered what to do with her and then the invitation arrived. Bummer!

After that, we were not in fear anymore, also nothing was felt at our street.

At 10:00, a man who was sent by a friend of Barbara came to get her out of here because all of the Jews will be taken away, from house to house. At this point, I was shaking in a way I never had before. Therefore, we decided that B. will stay here because we said either the stamping helps, or it does not, and we believed it will. In case that they will act according to the lists, Barbara has to be here. She got dressed really to leave and in that form she also went to bed. We went to bed as well. Nothing happened with us. And this morning, the facts: The targets this time were mainly the family members of men who are at Dutch labor camps. All had to go. The operation was horrifying and lasted from 7:00 in the evening to 4:00 in the morning. The participants were the W.M. , N.S.B (Dutch fascists), *Blacks, and the Hitler youth. Mercilessly, they took away thousands from their homes, toddlers and mothers, the old and the sick. We ran to two friends who were classmates of Sanne, the houses were empty! One of them came last night to return a book because they had heard that this time it is about their group. They say it will last today and tomorrow in all of the Netherlands. They say some are being sent to the big new camp that was erected in *Vught, but I do not know for sure.

About your papers, Franz wants to check tomorrow, he already filed a question regarding the matter in the past.

We were happy to read Hans' postcard. I hope that this way we can all evade! I am full of admiration for you being able to work so well.

Thousands of embraces to you and Lientje,

    Yours, Ilse.

- Blacks - The color of the uniform worn by the Dutch fascists
- Vught - concentration camp 50 Km south east of Rotterdam

October 17th, 42

Dear Paul and Lientje, I am returning you Paul's scarf as he had forgotten it here.

It was a lovely that he managed to arrive. I hope that he had been stamped well. Meanwhile, they wrote in the paper on the matter of *evicting the shoreline. Children! If this goes into action we cannot predict what consequences this will have on millions of people. Does this idea deeply affect you or will you sit silently waiting for things to come? We immediately thought of you but I still hope that you can stay there until the end of the winter. Franz' birthday was much more festive than we had imagined. Though we were very shocked from the fact that Max Bollela (head of the Y.R.) was arrested along with his family, probably being told about due to the stamping situation – but besides that, more guests arrived than expected, mom was here all day, even Tata (mom-grandma's old sister) was not flinched by the road. The photograph that Paul took of Paulien keeps making us happy. Even the girls feel so well with Paul. Barbara always claims that he is the only person who understands her... At the moment she lives her life completely separately from us along with her boyfriend, to whom she is very attached, but that is how it is supposed to be.

To the both of you, with Paulien, many embraces

    Yours, Ilse.

My dear,

Many thanks to you for the warm blessings for my birthday. I have a distinct feeling that your blessings will come true.

It was a very encouraging day and it turned out that I still receive a lot of friends which surprised and touched me.

It was very refreshing to be allowed to pat Paul shoulder again. It should happen more often! A loving greeting to all of you, Franz.

- Evacuation of all Jews from the coastal areas in Holland to the Amsterdam ghetto

18.11.42

My beloved children!

Stop worrying about us so much. So far, everything went well for us, even when we had guests for the fourth time yesterday, 10 minutes before midnight. They actually came to Mrs. De-Laub. All three men who came were overall decent men. I asked them to wait for a moment, to prepare the lady lying in bed because she is suffering from breast cancer. They immediately gave up, asked for the medical certificate and left her alone. They showed great interest in our portrait in my room. "This is you, Ma'am. It must have been made by a very good painter". They were also interested in a photograph of the Ledermanns and everything that was hanging in my room, they liked! I lost my fountain pen and hope to find it. How is Paulien? Does she still have fever? And what did the doctor say? Give her a warm kiss from me. We should hope that, soon, she will return to being healthy and cheerful.

My postcard crossed your lovely letter. It is a pity, what happened with your house, but maybe that will sort out soon as well. Hope it will not last much longer! Children, I am very tired but I do not dare lay in bed before 1:00 at night in case we have guests again. I must be ready to open the door.

Since Mrs. Von-Prague had guests last week, I do not take off my clothes before 2:00 at night, sometimes only at 4:00 in the morning, because I sink into sleep, broken down from fatigue as I do now. Phil and Ari are very unfortunate for having to leave their houses and children. They will probably suffer from great loneliness. It is hard for me, as well, to understand why Hans did not warn you, I thought this might happen to you. Seemingly unintentional forgetfulness, Lientje, do not pay attention to it. I am very excited towards your visit and embrace the three of you with all my heart.

I wish fast recuperation for Paulien, much love and also greetings from Tata and Lala.

    *Mom

• Mom – Ellen, Paul Ilse and Hans Mother

Amsterdam, November 19th, 1942

Dear Paul and Lientje,

Many thanks for your last two letters and from you, Paul, for the generous gift from the rich uncle to his cousins. It was a nice idea on your behalf, they are excited and would like to write to you tomorrow.

Contrary to that, I am writing right away out of distrust said tomorrow.

Lientje participations in our sorrow always annoy me a little because I am not that worried about us, I do not believe they will come so fast to take us away and in general look at oncoming completely peacefully. What needs to come will come eventually, if so, why be excited? I still enjoy the house, the family life and the cat, we should look forward to the transfer to the Transual area (the ghetto planned in Amsterdam) the most. Every day, more families are receiving an order to move there, mainly people living in our area. The time limit given for performing the transfer is between 4 to 8 days and they say we can take everything with us. It was said that everyone who received their stamping last, will be the first to receive the order of transfer, and since we were among the first to be stamped, there is a chance that this will take a while.

However, they already visited mom again on the evening of the day before yesterday, this time, because of "The old lady" Mrs. De-Lau. But they only took the medical certificate with them. They also revisited a number of other rooms, they even walked upstairs towards Arena's room and also peeked into Tata's room, were probably so frightened that they fled it fast.

The final finding: three young and extremely beautiful men that excitingly reviewed all of the photographs in mom's room, were amazed by the similarities of the oil painting made by Paul for mom and asked her about it. Mom told them than her son made it. They had also found an album of Ruth's on top of the closet and looked through it with great interest. It seems that the goal this time was only certificates, although they did not reject the belloni sandwich that mom gave them at the end. According to mom, they appeared at 11:30 at night, according to Arena, at 12:30 at night, and according to Mrs. Von Den Berg, at 01:30 in the morning.

It was the fourth visit, hopefully a fifth visit will not occur for now or that it will go by as nicely as this one did. Mom is already experienced by now but not everyone would hold up the way she does. Barbara talked about the husband of Haya (the dancer Haya Goldstein) today. It was said that he is an in isolated prison and does not receive any kind of food pretty much, he is in such bad mental health that they worry for his life.

It is hard to say if the general situation is a positive one or not. I hope and believe it is. And that is pretty much it! Write again soon and stay at your house for as long as possible, as it is not good to go out of your "element" (Hebrew word play for "house"). Thousands of wishes to the three of you and more thanks to Paul for the generous Santa Claus present.

    From the bottom of my heart, Ilse.

1.12.42

Dear Paul and Lientje,

Everything is well here as well. On Friday, during the course of the day, there was another big razzia.

Out of 900 that were gathered, 300 were again released later on, mostly those who work for the Wehrmacht and were gathered along with their families. Unfortunately, they had also taken Keita

Citroen child, who is 15 years old and worked for the fur-clothing manufacturer.

We very much enjoyed Paulien letter. Sanne immediately thought of replying but the letter stayed laying here.

Franz is so desperate that he is unapproachable.

    1000 Blessings, From Ilse.

Hans' address: The Daffodils Hotel, Montreux Switzerland.

December, 1942

Dear Paulien,

You are at luck again as only a girl who's name starts with P, A, U, and ends with L, Y, N, N, K, A may be because when I received your uplifting letter, I was just in the mood to write one. And so, I sat down and reached my hand out for a pen... Do you notice this writing paper? I received it from aunt Lala. When it is for you, nothing is good enough for me! (If you were here right now, I would have pressed you against my chest happily, but it is not shown at the moment because you are not here, and neither is my chest). So you see? It is so much fun for you to have a German language teacher that does not know German well! Ours does, but I do not! That is how it is! A dishonor to the entire family whose name I carry, with such fathers, in the past and present, when I receive a 6 in German, in my diploma. Right now we have a sort of a free hour on Wednesday afternoons, where we can also play ping-pong. Gabby is no longer staying with us, she came back to the Goslar family. The book did not arrive yet and the longing for this truly lovely book is untamable... Well, my cousin will still thank you for writing with a hand-shake, with a kiss, with warm family blessings, with a thank you to aunt Lynn with a kiss, for her letter I sign,

    Yours, Sanne.

P.S. From now on, I forbid you to fall sick without my permission, understand?

    Sanne.

Dear Uncle Paul, You saved me from great distress! (You did not know that, right?) Because when your great gift arrived, I had just wasted my last pennies buying ice cream with five. And now I will be able to buy Hanukkah gifts for my parents + Barbara + grandma + the big aunts. My older sister has a boyfriend now and I will have to buy him something as well, but he is actually a nice guy. We will manage. I will buy each one a packet of candies and will be done with it. A rich uncle is a good thing! I never had a "my rich uncle from Wassenaar " before – rings nicely, huh?

Today I did not go to school for the possibility of "razzia" (an operation of dispatching Jews for delivery), Of course nothing happened, but there was excitement and therefore.. Our school has to relocate. Maybe as early as tomorrow. Then we will be transferred to the high school building. In my opinion, our school has to be our school. We all hate the high school. It will be nice! Now I do not know if to go to my old school tomorrow (which returns to the municipality) or to the new one. I think of going to the old one first. If I will be late to the new one, I will not be punished (an exceptional case). Now so long and good bye,

      Sanne.

Part of Sanne Letter

Lieve Paubrencke.

Jij bofs maar weer zoals alleen een kind boffen kan, wiens naam begint met de letters P, A, U, en wiens naam eindigt met de letters L, I, E, N, E, K, en E. Want toen jij ik je welhei, den de brief ontving, had ik net zin om een brief te schrijven. En dus zette ik mij neer en greep naar de pen?....
Zie je dit postpapier? Van tante Lalla. Voor jou is me niets goed genoeg! (Als je nou hier was, drukte ik je smartelijk tegen mijn boezem, maar dat kan nu niet, want jij bent er niet en m'n boezem ook niet). Zo zie je weer!
Wat een bof, dat jullie een leraar voor Duits hebben, die geen Duits kan! Onze

14.12.42

My beloved firstborn and two lovely ladies, together you are such a one beautiful whole!

In the end I managed to find a delivery person to bring you the birthday cake that I baked.

I embrace each and every one of you with all my heart. I will not describe all the blessings in my heart because you know what they are. Only this one: That we will never have to celebrate this day separately. Though, it is very strange to me that I am not currently making preparations as I did in the past so that I could come over and spend the day together in the beautiful harmony of years gone by. I should not cry that it is over, but smile for that they happened and with great hope that they will come back.

If so, here you are, the three of you, lying in bed early in the morning, Paulien does not have the patience to wait until she is allowed to enter the room with her gifts and when dad stopped cheering and being impressed enough, mom reached her hand toward under the bed and like a magician pulls out her gift and apparently is Paul lying there empty handed either. Everyone gets their share and the embraces start over. Oh, it is so nice to describe all of this, and you were right my son, we appreciate the good that we have left twice as much.

I am bringing the cake soon to Bendeen and hope that it won't be too hard for Panky to bring you the bottle that is meant for you. If everything does arrive, then cheers to you and your friends.

I am certain that as per usual the guests will arrive in the evening, after the meal, and maybe even loyal Pitsha can free himself. How are things now with Ari? Please pass my regards to them and to the Charlottes and Mayers…

I managed to pass Ruth's and Hans' letters to Franz who surprisingly appeared that same day, so you may have already received them. Please send me mine so I can reply to it. It was made apparent that eventually they had to rearrange their lives a bit differently than they imagined, but everything seemed too dreamy for them, so it is not easy for them. But any closeness is better for freedom and security.

That is it, my beloved three, this is supposed to be a birthday letter which I am ending with a strong embrace.

    With all my love, Yours, Mom.

January 20th, 1943

My Dear,

We are not at peace because of mom and Tata. An action has begun against the guesthouses. A large amount of whom had already been emptied. Last night, an acquaintance of mom's came and told us in her name that her daughter is in line for today. She was very restless and did not know what to do. This operation lasted throughout the day. Therefore, she wanted to leave the house early in the morning only to return in the evening. At first, we agreed, but later that night, we had passed her a letter via messenger, in which we expressed our objections. We were worried that if we were to leave the house unattended during the day, it would have been broken into and later on signed off, and they will no longer have a place to go. She had returned our messenger with a very despaired letter, in which she wrote that she had heard that whoever is being taken anyway during the day, is immediately sent away to Vught, and from there, straight to Germany or Poland. She does not know what to do anymore but hopes that tomorrow everything will be clearer. Today, before noon, it was made known that today's operation is not aimed at all at guesthouses, but rather against all the people who, in the past, had received a postponing due to the condition of their health (their illness). Anywhere, as well as in our street, vehicles appeared, and the old and the sick people were taken out of the houses, some were carried out. It was a frightening sight. In the afternoon, we came to her place, Ilse and I, but they would not open the door for us and an acquaintance told us that everyone had left the house. Ilse found out later that mom and Tata were home but did not hear the doorbell. Ilse spoke with her. We do not know what to advise her. Some advice to stay in the house and some, to leave it during the day. They say that if they do take her during the day, there is nothing to be done about it, but, if they take her during the evening, she is brought to the center of the Jewish community and from there she may be released based on her stamping. There is speculation that tomorrow there will not be an action, but the day after, there will be. In addition to everyone there, that she have no help anymore.

Arena was taken and she sits at Westerbork. Another helper for daily work, Mrs. Gotshalk, does not dare coming anymore, as all of the workers of the guesthouses, all of whom fled.

So you can imagine the situation. Even you will not be able to help, but we wanted you to at least be in the picture. During the evening, the Jewish workers of the Wehrmacht are now always being gathered. At the moment I was writing this, Mrs. Tsiglenick came to our door and told us they are being taken away and that they are leaving. This is the third time they are being taken away, except that they were in a prison in Germany for 6 weeks, and we are very afraid that this time, they will not return.

    Yours, Franz.

My dear, soon I will not bear anymore! The physical and mental tolls are too great! I cannot see any more salvation for mom. I helped her pack. Everything is ready. Last night, only she and Tata stayed at home, the rest are gone.

    Ilse.

January 28th, 43

My dear, our letter to Mrs. Pordemberga was written just in time. Since last night mom is sitting at *Schouwburg (the house of the Jewish community of Amsterdam) along with all the residents of her guesthouse, including Lala. Johan and Lena came, at random, exactly 2 minutes after the Blacks came in (The color of the uniform worn by the Dutch fascists) there at 9:00 in the evening. They helped everyone pack until 11:30 in the evening, when everyone left. The bus came so late as he could not find the way due to the darkness. Johan called us at 9:30. We immediately notified *Prof. Cohen and Mrs. Pordemberga by phone. I was at the expo. with her first thing in the morning. Last night, she took action right after receiving the message, spoke about it with Slotzker and promised all the help. But today, no one had been released yet, but no one else did either. They will stay at Schouwburg tonight. They took a lot of food with them and are receiving a very good treatment. I sent her a message to Schouwburg, and candy, and mom replied that she is rather calm, so is Tata, who initially became nervous. Only that Tata is very hopeless. I am sure that mom will come back. The Tsiglenicks came back as well. Now we must wait again. What is worse is that Heinz wrote to us from the prison in Arnhem. He got caught! We have no more information about him. He wrote that he was not permitted to take anything with him and is asking for the most basic things such as a tooth brush, a shaving instrument, and clothes. We already sent everything. We know nothing about Eva.

Children! What a life! Lena says that mom is a wonder. She was very quiet and the entire time, was saying that I will return. Helped everyone and kept them calm.

• Schouwburg - Dutch theatre in Amsterdam where the Jews gathered by the Nazis before being sent (Now a museum).

• Prof. Cohen and Mrs. Pordemberga - Judenrat Workers (Prof. David Cohen was the head of the Judenrat with Mr. Abraham Asscher).

29. 1.43

This morning your letter and the news that Mrs. Von De Berg, Mrs. De Lau and De Paris are being released. Mom looked forward to it as well and was already standing dressed and ready, but there was a last minute disruption. Not clear why. I was at the expo. They are vigorously working on the case and hoping to release her today. The main thing is that they are staying in Schouwburg until Tuesday. Oh, children!

Heinz already arrived in Westerbork, Eva is ok except being nervous, she is not focused. We are doing everything in our power to keep Heinz there.

Children! She was <u>released</u>! I am arriving from the expo. right now. There, I was told that mom and the two sisters were already on the way to the train towards Westerbork with the old and the sick, that Slotzker drove there especially for her, so far without result but will try again at 6 o'clock. I was completely hopeless and right now I got home and Franz told me she got out of there! She called by phone and said she is at a nursery by Schouwburg and will stay there for the night. We are already heading there.

    Yours, Ilse.

• A postcard from grandma (Ellen) to Paul, after the first imprisonment - back to Amsterdam – At Ilse's house.

1.2.1943

Beloved children, here I am again, unfortunately without Tata and Lala (her two sisters).

It is a terrible thing, but I had to make a choice: them or you. Ilse just arrived to take me from the hostel where I had to spend the night. My legs and the rest of me – were so drained that I could in no way come here by foot. Ilse called for an ambulance and here I am since yesterday at 12:30, at the Ledermanns. I was so tired and broken from the pain in all my limbs that I cannot do anything at all. It was luck that Hugh and Lena came for me at the right time. They helped us and called all sorts of authorities. That way, the night went by completely differently than we imagined when I invited them over. The neighbors came to lend a hand until we were finally ready to leave, they waved at us, said their goodbyes and cheered for us. Yes, and the two poor sisters? I cannot free myself from thoughts about them. Tata was completely confused and maybe thanks to that she will not see what is happening. Farewell my three beloved! Embraces!

And a lot of love, From Mom and Hal.

Remark added latter probably by Ilse - (On the 8th of February, about a week after being released with great efforts, she (Ellen) walked into her empty apartment for a few moments to take a few belongings. Shortly after, at 17:00 in the afternoon, the Fascist commando came to take her, she was at first brought to Schouwburg – the Amsterdam theatre that became the first gathering area at the time, from there, people were sent to camps in the Netherlands or straight to Auschwitz, she was sent to camp Westerbork in the Netherlands, near the German border).

3.2.43

Beloved Lientje and Paul!
You want to know how all of this happened. As you know, I invited Lena and Johan for a cup of tea at 9 o'clock exactly a week ago. Everything in the kitchen was ready as they like to, when the doorbell is being

rang three times. Are they here yet? I opened the small window of the entrance door "Who is there?" the police. I open "We came to take away Mrs. Schonlicht-Phillips." I do not know one", I replied. "Is that so? But she is supposed to live here! And who are you? Show your identification certificate!" – "that is the same Phillips." No, I say, "here you can see, it says *Phillippi". "Who else lives here? We must see all of the identification certificates." I opened the doors of all the rooms and they asked each one if her name was Schonlicht-Phillips and I was asked again if such lady lived here in the past, it seems that the intention was for Phillipe and whoever lived upstairs, because they had an order for one named Noyman-Phillips. They had to take <u>everyone</u> away and <u>I had</u> to make sure everyone would be ready within 3/4 of an hour. You can imagine my heartbeat. Meanwhile, 5 minutes after the police, came Lena, and later on Johan. He immediately called Franz and the expositor, as well as influential acquaintances of the rest of my guests. Lena packed all the food items she could get for me, one of the sisters Mrs. P. Lala's house owner, came to say that Lala was not obligated to join because she cannot walk. I accompanied Mrs. P. to say goodbye to Lala. Mrs. Pen Prague was also released from the journey because her daughter is ill with breast cancer, but the next day they said, when they come to check if the houses are empty, that they will take the sick as well, with stretchers. And so, since this was said, everyone decided to join immediately.

Good neighbors came to help everyone pack. Finally, at 11:30 we were boarded onto a truck, where 2 people were already inside, and on the way 3 more were added, and we were brought to Schouwburg. We arrived there at about 12 o'clock at night, signed up, and the big luggage was taken for keeping. Everyone was left with all the small packages, small suitcases, backpacks, bags etc. We were looking for a seat on one of the nine very long benches and that is how we spent the first night after coffee that was given out to everyone present (about 300 people). My people behaved just fine, and I was sure I would be released and so I was in good spirits, which somewhat affected the others.

Everyone who had a chance to be released or receive a stamping that postpones the gathering, were obligated to give their identification certificates the next morning. I cannot describe the multitude of disappointment that I felt when three of us were released and I was not among them. Everything turned upside down and I did not know who I am from all the fear and the horrible pain that came with the thought of not seeing everyone ever again and that I had to leave you all without saying goodbye. Whoever was left was divided, the young people to Vught, the old to Westerbork. The latter, that also included us, were sent to the exit (of the theatre hall) and there we had to spend the second night without any sort of comfort. Of course, we sank into sleep anyway and woke up on and off with pain in our limbs. At 9:30, we were again given coffee and 6 sandwiches with jam, and at 12, the trucks (who brought us earlier with all our items), were waiting for us again, brought us 2 To the train that leaves for Westerbork, though only at 8:00 in the evening so it arrives at 01:30 in the morning. I could not contain myself, although I was surrounded by brothers to the same misfortune I could not stop the tears when thinking of you. While we were sitting for about 2 hours on the train, I heard my name being called. I was taken off the train and you know the rest! But the drama did not stop. Through the Y.R. we were told Lala's shed number is 69, she asked us to send her a mug and food and we already sent her a package. Nothing about Tata. And tonight we found out that one of them and maybe both will be sent straight onwards. How will they be able to put up with that? The thought is unbearable. The time currently is 12:30 and going to sleep is unacceptable. The only thing that can be wished for them is that everything ends fast and that they will not have time to understand their fate. How sad is it that there is a necessity to wish such a thing!

Lientje, are you feeling better and is the operation behind you? I am very calmed knowing Johanna is with you, so you could at least heal well, send her my warm regards. To you and Paulien, much love and embrace from Mom

• Ellen former last name was Philippi

4.2. 43

Good morning children, the night passed and the time is 7 o'clock in the morning. Well, I managed to sleep for a few hours and that is more than I expected. The cat is sitting on the table and strokes my letter with his white leg, he especially fancies ink that has not dried out yet, and he is now lying peacefully on my knees. He is the whole family's spoiled pet and is used as distraction. I, of course, enjoy being here but I will need to make an effort to find a room for myself. I hope to find a room around here so to not risk anyone here in the house, because I had not been called out yet to sort my papers. I am only allowed to take necessities for my daily needs, from my house to my future house. In any case, I cannot do much besides helping with Ilse's household chores, who shows undeniable diligence and efficiency. On any spare moment, she is busy helping other, she is not familiar with the meaning of rest. She does everything silently and with her thought put into it. Franz seems unwell and of course very worried about everything that is going on. Yes, our lives are not easy right now. Everyone is still asleep, therefore, I am sending warm regards from everyone. Kisses from Mom.

P.S. At Schouwburg, we were given acceptable food: soup and cooked vegetables.

4.2.43

Dear children, poor Lientje,

I had not written anything at all regarding the matter of your teeth. I am glad that the surgery went well and hope you will heal up fast. Do you know that my head is spinning from all the distress around me and everything else that I still need to arrange for mom. If we will not find her a room soon, they will take out everything she has in her house, before she is able to salvage anything. But that is a small part of our worries. It seems that Heinz's situation (Franz' brother in law, Ray Campepper's father) regarding the deportation is very unclear, although it is fortunate that he is no longer punishable.

Mom is still in a post stroke condition at the moment, looks like a small old lady, I hope she will recover.

The thought of Tata and Lala is maddening. And to think that mom was saved from the same fate at the last moment. Did you thank Mrs. Pordemberga?? She did her very best and was excellent in her way of treating this whole case.

I am very grateful to her and all of the expositor's work that treated it as if it was the only case. Franz wrote a great letter to Slotzker.

The books you sent gave us great pleasure and it had probably been two weeks since I sent them forward. It was at exactly that time that three people were standing at the mail room and gave the following addresses for the packages delivery:

Westerbork, Oranienburg concentration camp, *St. Michiels Gestle. Today's Europe! As I am writing you these lines, someone is yelling down the street: "three, four!" And the soldiers begin to sing. God! When will this nightmare end?!

Embraces to everyone and full healing for all the teeth.

    Yours, Ilse.

The painting of the flowers that belonged to Tata is hanging in my room.

• St. Michiels Gestle (St. Michielsgestel) is where Vught concentration camp located about 50 Km south east of Rotterdam.

Ellen Citroen Deportation to Westerbork

Tuesday, 9.2.43

My dear, Paul and Lientje,

Last night I thought I could no longer bear this and was left hopeless, but today a spark of trust has returned, maybe Slotzker will manage to sort the situation a second time. Starting yesterday at 6:00 in the afternoon, mom has been sitting at Schouwburg again. At about 4:30 she went to her apartment, something that made me feel terrible the whole time, but she really wanted to and so at 6:30 the daughter of the dentist, Mr. Katz, came and told me that mom was taken out of the apartment.

She saw a car of the commando pull by her house and one "green" (a German commando soldier) ringing mom's door. Apparently, she opened up and shortly after left the house with him and got into the car. Katz immediately ran to the expositor because he knows Slotzker personally and she (the daughter) came to us. With my hands shaking, I quickly packed mom's small suitcase and with the addition of two blankets and with the company of Laticia Katz, brought everything to the expo. Franz got there by bicycle. There was only one man there who said that mom is surely already on the train that leaves at 8:00. The time was 7:00! I asked to bring the belongings there. He also thought that they will still try to release her at the train station. When, by 9:00 there were still no news of her, I imagined her already at Westerbork or on the way there, I phrased an appeal in writing where I described her services during the First World War in detail, so she would at least arrive to Theresienstadt. This morning, an acquaintance from the expo., Miss Boll, appeared, who said that at 9:00 in the evening, mom was still in Schouwburg, that is what she heard from Mr. S, who saw mom there last time as well. I was hopeful again. I immediately ran to Mr. S, home, he thought that someone ratted about mom when she was at the apartment. I did not think of such thing earlier. I thought she went towards her fate when she entered the apartment right at the time they were looking for someone specific there, I ran to the expo with 2 packages and a letter for mom and asked the man who was meant to pass her the items to ask her why she is there and how all of this happened. While I was waiting for him to come back, I saw by chance, Slotzker exiting, I walked up to him and said "I am Mrs. L., my mom is at Schouwburg". He said "Mrs. Citroen? Why did she go to her apartment? She should have sent someone else!" He was very angry. "I will see what I can do." He said that this is not a punishable case because there was nothing else to do and I assume that mom is on the list of the guesthouses again and the luggage is gone! All of her warm things are gone. A telegram was immediately sent to Westerbork but I have no hope that the luggage will be found. Which worries me very much. Where will I quickly find everything that she needs, will the luggage truly be sent? All of her toiletries, her house slippers etc. But I am still hopeful. Mr. Symon promised to go back to Schouwburg at 3:00 o'clock and try to speak with the official that arrested her because he knows him well and point out the mistake since mom was just released. Let him succeed! God! She was so exhausted and tired and so warm and kind; and I was really happy with her and that I could properly take care of her here at my house. And we worked so well together. I had never ever received such a shock. Like the one at the moment they came to tell me those dreadful news. At first I could not understand a thing.

9:30. At 5:00, a message was received from mom that she needs certain things since a cargo left at night towards Vught. I immediately packed the most utter necessities out of our belongings into a small suitcase and rolled a covered duvet, a pillow and a robe with lining. These I sent to Schouwburg. I gave away the boots and her umbrella when I was there. Across from there, at the hostel, I was told there was still definitely a chance, everyone knows the case – but the releases are only being performed shortly before the departure of the train at 2:00 in the morning. If so, maybe 12 or 1 at night and we must continue and count on Slotzker's ability. When I arrived home tonight, another message arrived from mom that she is hoping to see us again soon. She received the morning's delivery and everything in good condition. The man with whom I sent the items said that mom definitely fell victim to a miserable coincidence. Yesterday, all of the guesthouses were checked to make sure no one stayed, that is how they found mom and took her with them. So it is a coincidence.

Children, I will not bear losing her over such lightheadedness.

Wednesday morning.

Everything is over! She was sent to Vught, will probably arrive at Westerbork. We already started doing everything we can to make her stay easier. It is horrible. I cannot bear this. She could have been sitting here right now and enjoy herself. She is gone solely for silly recklessness. We could have thought about that: on Mondays, Wednesdays, and Fridays, the days of the arrests, we should not allow her to go there. But who would have thought that they would go there again, where everything was already emptied.

Mrs. Von-Prague is still in Westerbork with her daughter.

I am sending a food package to P. by our friend from there, Mr. Lehman. If she is still there, he will pass it to her. I have received your letter, Lientje. Rein already brought everything.

    Yours, Ilse.

12.2.43

My dear, thank you for the lovely letter. Lientje, mom wore a shirt, a wool sweater and also your knitted sweater. Before she went out I told her that it is very cold outside and therefore she wore your upper sweater. Warm house slippers, if they have a leather sole, are welcome, Yesterday I bought her a pair of gloves made out of very thick wool. Also welcome are: warm socks, a shirt, a pair of pants, but there is no need in the brown coat. I bought her another suitcase and I wish to send it to her quickly in Westerbork along with everything. There, we have a friend from the Y.R. that will make sure to hand it over to mom when she arrives. We have no news whatsoever. There are no mailing service to Vught so I have heard this morning when I sent 2 letters there. I also sent 2 food packages that should arrive. You are also allowed to send 15 florins per week, but she still has money left. At the moment I have no clue regarding when she will leave that place or maybe she had already left or she may stay there. The lack of information is intolerable.

Maybe it is best that you send the items to Haya or to Vachtel, or as I did, to Miss Lissel Austreicher of the Y.R. .

The current address is: Ellen Citroen- Philippi, date of birth - 30.6.72, delivery from the - 10.2.43, reception camp Vught. If you are sending the items you should of course mention the recipient but not <u>inside</u> the package, because that is forbidden, but rather separately.

They have also caught Heinu Held, along with hundreds of others.

      With affection, Ilse.

17.2.43 in the evening

My Paulien and Lientje,

Mr. Bleete returned and brought a note from Leihman with him which seemingly been dictated by mom and says: "the treatment is ok. The luggage did not arrive. Greetings to the children". If the luggage was sent to Schouwburg, it was lost as well and she was left with nothing! That is just unacceptable! Without a blanket, without anything. I feel like screaming. I am certain she will receive help because besides Leihman who will certainly take care of her, there are more acquaintances there. Tomorrow I will file a complaint but how will that help. Do you have any more bathing napkins? I do not. Today I sent another food package to Vught because on Tuesday she was still there, but I do not dare sending more clothes because she could arrive in Westerbork any day so they say here and so I believe. I will now send two additional blankets to Westerbork. The rest is in the suitcase that I already sent there and did not yet receive a confirmation that it arrived. I would like to send a few more items, Tata's warm robe was also in that bundle among with the duvet and the pillow. And the good edible things were at the small suitcase and I thought she would at least enjoy that. How can we hold on, how?...

I cannot write to Hans. Maybe you will do that? And I am sending you another letter from Peter Diamant, maybe you can take care of that, at the moment I cannot put my mind into these things.

Keep the letter from Hans, when mom arrives in Westerbork we will send it to her as well as the photograph. God, characters from another world! Does that still exist? And generally speaking, send mother a few photographs from you because all of the photographs were also in the suitcase that was lost.

Yesterday afternoon I passed by mom's house. Everything had already been emptied. Miss P. said that the Germans took 7 trucks' worth of items from there. Inside her room, on the wall, remained the photograph of the three of you. Books, boxes of photographs and papers were carelessly scattered on the floor... they have no need for those. Only to stop thinking.

If you have newer photographs of Hans, send her those as well.

Thousands of greetings to you, Ilse.

18.2.43

Paulien, I should never have driven you mad as well, Franz visited the place where I had given the luggage for Schouwburg today. They had a note with mom's personal signature in which she stated that she received the small suitcase and the bundle of blankets. If so, she definitely received the luggage. She must have meant that what I had given on the first evening at the expo did not reach her, because it was sent directly to Westerbork.

Children, a heavy weight got off my chest. Today I sent another food package and added 2 blankets and 1 spoon as well. Heinz is still in Westerbork. He returned us our wind coat and 2 shirts because he received some of his clothes.

Farewell children,

>Yours, Ilse.

23.2.43

Paulien, Lientje, I am so happy. There are some good news from Westerbork, not from mom herself but through our friends. The most important one is that one person wrote this to his parents: "Heinz K. told me that there is nothing to worry about regarding Ilse's mom for now." (Meaning: there is no immediate danger that she will be sent onward…) so it seems that our softening works were still fruitful and of course Haya has a big part in that, they say that she is very influential there. Your job is to continue grooming her case.

I was so restless all day, I thought maybe today she is already gone.

I am so happy. Later on someone wrote that mom is so brave, that she drank coffee with her, and that I should send sheets and a pillow, something I already did. Her position is admirable by everybody. And another miracle happened: the small suitcase and the 2 blankets that were accidentally sent to Westerbork back then were found and handed over to mom. Now she is set and can choose what she will take with her and what she will leave there. This is what happiness looks like these days! Etty Prince writes to me that Rou Prince and her husband suddenly appeared there at a penalty shipment. And Etty's father, old Morforego arrived as well and was sent onwards. She was sitting in quarantine over a few cases of Diphtheria and could barely speak with him.

Today they came to take Anne's parents, the old Putshnik. They lived on the Merwedeplein and the whole family is now gone. The old and sick gathering operation continues rapidly, day and night.

If so, you can now write to mom as much as you would like but carefully. And you can also send treats. It was written to me that she now has everything so now it is about genuinely heart-warming things. If Paulien will make her a drawing or something of that sort.

People, people, if we can only hold her there for some time longer, at least until the coldest season passes.

Farewell, farewell, with great affection, Ilse

I did not receive the books yet.

1.3.43

A postcard from grandma, which was sent from Westerbork to Paul.

A. Citroen- Philippi, Camp Westerbork Barrack 64

My beloved children! I was welcomed so nicely by all our friends and your friends and the beautiful package was waiting for me as well! Haya was the first and yesterday, Sunday, I was invited to drink coffee with her at Dr. Wallach's place. If only all of this would not be happening here, it would have been a great pleasure. – It was nice but missing all of you... is unbearable.

Tomorrow the journey will continue, the train is standing ready. We will only know who will need to go at 4:30 in the morning. I do not have a lot of hope. Thank you for <u>everything</u>. Teach Paulien not to forget me. You live inside me, and for you I exist.

    Be blessed, Mom

3.3.43

"Dear Ledermanns, I am passing you greeting from Heinz and Manorey, they are both well. Noori was happy to receive a pair of shoes because she only had the pair she was already wearing. The pair that was wrapped in the blanket bundle was gone. She would also like the suede shirt that you currently have. Today I received a package as well did Lizzel.

On Sunday, our first "campers" will arrive, I assume that Hans Bale will be among them. That way you can receive fresh news verbally. From the house, they wrote to us that everything else is a reason for high spirits, and for that we are very happy, despite everything.

Kindly yours, Hilda Kramer.

I have no idea how to get a pair of shoes, size 37, or 38 probably. Do you have an idea? Lientje, do not get mad at me but I am so exhausted right now, physically and mentally, I feel that I do not have the strength to host Paulien for the night. I do not have an extra bed because I gave it to a man whose house was completely emptied. And so Paulien will need to sleep on the sofa in the front room, it's not pleasant for her and for myself and it causes an effort to offer help and tidy up. All of these look like a mountain to me. Besides, this does not feel like a birthday to me, I had to think really hard over why you suddenly want to come visit specifically next Monday. I would love to see you and speak with you and you could hear what Bale is sharing, coming right out of his mouth. Maybe you should bring Paulien with you on Monday, although, she will not be able to meet Sanne because since she has a long day at school that includes the hours of noon as well.

I am including you a postcard that mom started writing in Schouwburg, continued in Vught when she waited for the continuation of the journey and eventually sent it from Westerbork. Atrocious! Please, return it to me and please send me the one she sent to you on March 1st so I could read it.

Thousands of greetings and love, Yours, Ilse.

Monday, 22nd of March 43, Westerbork

Lientje! Paul! Paulien! My dear,

The teeth has been taken care of and the shoes you sent makes me feel I am whole again and can appear in an orderly manner in front of you on your birthday. Although it will be different from years gone by where nothing could stop me from coming over with the traditional cake which included my warm embrace and all my blessings inside of it. This time we must be grateful for being at least able to communicate and must not lose hope that in upcoming years we can experience all the days' worth celebrating together, as per usual. My beloved, all of you, you spoil me so much. Your warm letters and packages full of love, at this irregular time, help bear the situation more easily and everyone takes part in them curiously.

Up until now, everything arrived without losses, as in Vught as in here, only one meat patty was missing from one of Ilse's package. I was compensated about that yesterday when the shoes arrived with an extra. With 3 well-fitting pairs of socks. Very comfortable and I am not bothered at all by the brown color. I am very pleased with them and can return you yours, Lientje, I wore them twice which did not damage them, the brush and the paste I will keep for my new shoes. The fruits are lovely, but kids, you are taking these from your plates. I already feel like a real "beggar". Yesterday I had another lovely afternoon with Heinz as well as last Sunday at Dr. Bale's, where I also met Mrs. Goldbaum who I did not know Ilse knew. When her relatives lived at my place on Beethoven st., I saw her quite often. From there I went to visit Haya who had received Ilse's letter.

She lives in a small room, along with one woman, and they would not let me leave.

I had to dine with them, it was very pleasant and so I only got back to my barrack at 8:00 o'clock, exactly as ordered. I found a note there, saying I need to go to Dr. V. I could not do it since it was already 5:00 o'clock so I will go today. Mrs. Landuar was at my place before she wrote to Ilse and also Mayers, they already seem "Westerbork possessed", meaning, somewhat tacky. I also notice many other acquaintances, though I do not make an effort to meet them because that would only disturb my thoughts of being with you. I am always waiting impatiently for news about Franz' health condition which Ilse loyally provides to me daily. Dr. B said that these illnesses became common recently but their origins are not clear yet. I can understand how much it depresses him. And you, Lientje, how is your waist pain, what did the doctor say? I hope and wish you to quickly heal up. Ilse, are you still without any help? It is unacceptable that you had to overcome all of this by yourself over time. And worrying over me is added up to that. Oh, children! My three girls, your letter makes me happier than I could describe, but Paulien is a little dictator, very funny, Paul, what you are writing about Paulien! Haya says that I remind her of you a lot. She sometimes says: "just like paul!"

My love, we are <u>together</u> and we will stay together!

Embraces from Mom.

Westerbork, 19.4.43

My beloved! Firstly, many many thanks again for the beautiful packages! Everything arrived in good condition, none of the glass was broken, and the flowers recovered fast in fresh water. They are standing in front of me and give me joy. Pauls' package and everyone's letters as well! Always surprises! When there will be jam again, Ilse, it is better to keep it in a mug rather than a paper cup, those often get crushed and that's a shame. I would also love to receive some kinds of grain, half of bread or pumpernickel as well. The size of the portions here became very small. We can no longer cook, they took the ovens. One was moved to the laundry corner so they could warm up baby food. There is also a long line of 42 water taps for about 300 woman in the barrack, many beds were added – and one emergency toilet for the night. Since the toilets flush is usually broken, we most of the time "enjoy" "the Westerbork scent". During the day, to answer these needs, the toilets barracks are equipped with 36 toilets. Every 9 of those are aligned in length and width, without partitions, as if an invitation to start conversations with neighbors. The blessed toilet paper is also used by me to mainly blow my wet nose.

I really needed new sheets, a bed sheet and a pillow case not too large in size. When you receive the bed sheet I sent back you will also receive an answer for your question regarding flees, luckily traces of them are left on the sheets and not on my body. On the contrary, I very much enjoy the sticky bandages (Band-Aids) to treat the burns I "acquired" in my struggle for a place near the space heater. The struggle with dust here is hopeless. It attacks clothes, blankets and everything underneath! Only a private experience can give a real idea of the life here. Indescribable. It is nice that at least the sun is spoiling us. Carrying around through the mud during rainy days is a very questionable pleasure. Now the list of my additional requests. I am very sorry for you, my Ilse, and also for myself because I have to weigh down on you a lot and quite often. But nothing else is allowed anymore, at least your letters will be kept, I cannot pass on them. They provide me with courage and endurance!

If so: Arena had her laundry brush stolen and she longs for another very much. One lady that helps me often, whose name is Tzillentzigger, would like a tea strainer like mine. Suspenders for Lenny K., she is laying in the hospital with respiratory inflammation. And for me a few more towels, so I could change up, I would also like you to return your wool pants to me. I washed it as you can see but I could not overcome the sand and the dust. I would also be happy with a piece of Sunlight soap.

Sophie and Bernard visited me a few times, I treated them with latkes accompanied by great fish spread and the grains with onion that they had were also very delicious. I fear for them very much. Lena and another B. Citroen were immediately sent onward. Last night, between 7 and a quarter to 8, I visited Mrs. Rosyn at the hospital, who is there with her mom but is not hospitalized herself. She is filled with restlessness and worries. I went to Dr. B to find out information for her, she already spoke with him herself – and I could go back to her with soothing news.

Mrs. Landaur came to the window in the morning, just as I was busy cleaning, I accompanied her to the hospital where she brought food for her mother. From there, to her husband who is lying in another barrack for the sick with very high blood pressure. Mrs. L was in terrible conflict since she and her husband were signed up for a shipment that is leaving today towards Theresienstadt. Thanks to the doctor's advice, their names were transferred to the next shipment. She was calmed by this and asked you to inform her sister of this. I met her again in evening at Mrs. R's, whose mother is very bad condition. Let's hope this will not take much longer. – Mrs. R. tells me that you, Franz, my dear, are back to being the way you were and that you are also looking well. For that I am very glad. You have no idea how much your words, even if they are numbered, cheer me up by being so understanding and full of your known humor. And how much Sanne is similar to you in that matter.

The lady praised you with the kindest words. Everyone who knows my children tells me how rich I am, as if I did not already know that myself. yes Lientje, you tell me about it as well, and coming from you I can accept it. Your package was again lovely, only one lemon was spoiled, the Ovaltine bread as well, or however it is called.

It was very delicious, but you did not say anything about yourself and Ilse wrote that you are still unwell, does it have to do with your aching waist? Apparently your social life is still very acting, if so, you do not seem to be suffering in the eyes of your acquaintances, and how could it? It is very hard to get to know Paulien, who is suddenly a big girl. Paul, are you pleased with Mr. Schroder's portrait? And is he? I had received this big spreadsheet from Dr. Vachtel. I do not see him often because he is very busy in his office, but his mood is always good.

Sanne, Helga is again very pleased with the little package but it is not that necessary. Hers and her parents' name, as I can see appears at least x6 a week on the list.

She sent her appreciation lately, in direction towards you as well as to the whole class. I would like to see Franz repairing socks again! After all, it is such help for you, Ilse. And it seems, Barbara, that you have blended well in engagements and that you are learning a lot of new things. I am glad that your classes are helping to distract you somewhat. Write whatever you would like to me, which is like I see you before me. have you heard from Hans? Many thanks to Tilly and Lizzie! And to all of you, many warm embraces from grandma-mom.

Heinz and Mrs. Levine were very pleased with the vegetables, and so was I of course!

    Ellen

6.5.43

My dear Paul and Lientje,

You spoil me so much! This Mocke, is it not that all of our childhood is buried in this. (Mocke, a renowned German artist, a good friend of Paul's who the same age as he is). Paul, I was crying at certain parts. I was very intensely involved in all of these, everything is going by, right in front of my eyes again very clearly as well as this spiritual wave and spun us both around at the time. But at the time, I did not understand the connection between the thing as I do now, I was also not aware that you knew Mocke from back at Brandenburg.

And in general, him being so eccentric came back to my mind. Man! You caused me such happiness! And Mayer and the "Storm" library and the storm itself, I was so involved in all of this, I grew up in this. Many thanks! And a special thanks you to Lientje for repairing the socks and the gentle work on the shirt. She made me just as happy, although in the nonetheless important materialistic field.

On the 23rd, Mrs. Rosyn, who meanwhile was sent onwards, wrote that "almost everyone looks good and fresh, mainly your mother. It cannot be compared with the weak, tired and thin woman, as I saw her last time at your place. Her cheeks are red, round, she is dressed beautifully and young, most people dress the way they feel about their stay here. Your mom is being supportive of me just as you are. She is great." Meanwhile I heard that a lot of people who had a stamping were sent from there, they are talking about 700, because too few people came from here.

Currently I am anxiously waiting for mail. I hope to receive something from Heinz these days.

It is very hard to obtain butter here, but I managed to send mom a quarter kilogram of margarine that was sent to us by an acquaintance from *Nijmegen. We do not have any plans but I am still not that worried about us. Barbara is well prepared now. Goodbye sweethearts,

    Yours, Ilse.

• City and province in the Netherlands close to the German border.

20.5.43

Paul and Lientje, my dear, thank you for the content of the letter and for the postcard.

Heinz wrote today that mom is taking care of the sick in her barrack and that it allows her to cook from time to time. She was lying down for a few days but she is back on her feet, although not everything is so well. She is fighting with all her power against the situation, she is brave and admirable. Hopefully she will not be sent specifically this time.

They say that even 80 of those with the red stampings were sent onwards. And those are considered the best ones!

Today, not only those who did not have stampings were arrested, that only few of whom appeared and that there is a big fear due to what might happen tomorrow, but also those who became Christians. There are many friends and acquaintances under that category, including Chris and Lizzie and her husband also got an order. But thanks to the hard work done by some people today, on L.'s birthday, they managed to get the stamp which got them out of this for now. The less sympathetic always succeed in operations such as this…

We should assume that this will not last much longer with us. My head is spinning. I hope that I will at least manage to arrange connections for mom. There is an exchange list for Palestine. Meaning, people who can prove that they have parents or children in Palestine. Or that they have a certificate, are signed up for the exchange and will be sent there in exchange of German citizens. Up to now, all of the people in Westerbork were held and were not sent onwards. Right now we are trying this through the Palestinian office in Geneva, to whom we could telegraph through the Red Cross.

They were interested about the number of our certificate while at Toby's in Tel Aviv. We asked Hans to push this forward but it is likely already too late. It will help if we will receive a confirmation letter from Palestinian office in Geneva. Now we are waiting.

Well, Pauls'. Much more love. You should be very happy that you are not living here.

1000 blessings, Ilse.

A few of the order receivers appeared – meaning disappeared – ran away – hid!!

The others, who complied with the order – were scared of the terrible outcome!

24.5.43

Beloved mother,

Yes! The turn of the Y.R. arrived on Friday, as I already mentioned, Cohen (the head of the Y.R) received a message that part of the Y.R. will be gathered for shipment for work in Germany. On Saturdays and Sundays they were working day and night on these lists. The Y.R was forced to write those lists and make sure the orders were shipped. It is despairing work. Some are forced to dig their own graves. On Sunday evening Barbara was on duty. At first only 50% of the young people were signed up and then they managed avoid signing her up. Later on the demand was suddenly 70%, so they came up to her crying and told her they are forced to sign her up. They offered her any help possible and told her she was one of the best workers. And, how did that help us? We went through a terrible night. Sunday morning, Franz went to the *keizersgracht to speak with Mayer De-Paris, he found out that he already managed to remove her name from the list. Franz collapsed from the stress. He collapsed on the neck of lady De-Langa who told him about that and sobbed. It seems that they are trying not to tear apart families as much as they can, especially when involving such a young girl. Boy, such torture will be caused to so many families today and tomorrow! It was said that 8,000 orders were sent. We are worried that due to the magnitude of the situation, only a few people will appear and those left will bear reprisals. In any case, everything should be prepared for departure, Moreover, we do not know if removal from lists will still be possible. It seems that Franz will be among the last ordered. Anyway, the situation is terrible, we are constantly worried and stressed.

Today I sent a package to Heinz, to which I added a few items for you. Mrs. Mahler came over on Saturday afternoon so I could read her your letter. The letter was at Paul's, but I knew it by heart.

The Mahlers need to head east right now!

Mom's letter is to this point. I am sending you a copy because I cannot rewrite everything again.

By the way, you are no longer allowed to send packages. Only Jews from Amsterdam are allowed, so send them to me.

You can in no way imagine what is being done here.

I passed forward Hans' postcard. Great! - today I invited the RSPCA to come and pick up our cat and bird so they could find them another home. I am scared of keeping them here. Our hearts are broken. But some things are worse.

With affection, Ilse.

• keizersgracht - Caesar Canal St.

14.6.43

Beloved children!

Hilda and Hans are on their way to you. I passed my greetings with both of them because at that moment, as per usual, I could not come up with anything else. I was at Hilda's myself for a few moments, Hans came over on Saturday as I was just about to go to bed, earlier than usual, because it was after work that started at 05:30 Friday morning and ended at 06:30 on Saturday morning. It was already forbidden to go to the hall so I could only ask them for some nice ribbon to tie my summer dress collar, made out of white lace or knitted.

Maybe such thing is still obtainable. In all of your packages, letters and deliveries I could once again find sources of joy, life, encouragement and mainly relaxation regarding you, the Ledermanns, I am solely worried about the Pauls' and hope that everything will remain the way it is. Paulien writings and drawing are again so lovely. It is so nice that the dolls remember me still as well but I do not forget them either. All the strength-giving medicine is of use to me more than ever, right after and as I was lying for days suffering from stomach contractions and over-exhaustion. I will have to listen to you, Franz, because my age is now felt although the body becomes stronger due to the current regimen conditions. After healing, a 25 hours work day caused me a lot of satisfaction. On Friday, at 7:00 in the evening, the barrack was cleared of everyone who arrived only 4 days earlier. The beds were taken out and the floor was cleaned, but not to much success.

Everything that was left, was scattered and forgotten, gathered and taken away and the area was prepared for the foreign citizens that were arrested 4 weeks ago, no one knows why, and are since then arrested in *Amersfoort. Most of these people lived at the Jewish Square in Amsterdam. It might be so that their parents migrated to the Netherlands many years ago, but in any case, they consider themselves special. Their hate towards the Jewish Germans is poisonous and uncontrollable.

Though I am not personally suffering from this, it is still painful. By the way, all of these look excellent and are full of praises regarding the treatment and order under the S.S. regimen in Amersfoort, contrary to here.

The first ones arrived here at about 3:00 at night, the last at 5:45. At 6:15 I went to sleep until 7:00 and then my daily work began: prepare the list of ill people at the men's and women's hall, which were separated by only the entrance to the barrack, a passage here that is called "kitchen". My job is to also bathe them if they are unable to do so by themselves, change bandages if needed, prepare them a porridge or tea etc. They get to know me quickly and know that they can always find me at my corner. If you are able to, add a few bandages with a width of 2 to 6 centimeters. We are not lacking hands, legs and wounded arms here, though I did receive good help, the help you, Sanne, are offering, I would be more than happy to

receive, though from time to time you can still help mom.

Dear Ilse, it is very exciting that you are still sending things to Eva at L. and to so many others about whom you are always thinking and sending exactly what is needed. I am in love with the mug with the lid that has the capacity of 1/2 liter and that was full and accompanied by so many good things, it is used for so many things. The mug with the angel on it was stolen from me, I would love to receive another, but it can also be a thick cup with a bottom. The china bowl arrived, sadly, though the good packaging, with broken nozzle and handle. It is still very useful, as is the pillow, for which may I please receive 2 covers? Am I allowed to give my sweatpants to someone else? There is huge demand for these things as there is for children's newspapers! At the moment, there is a large number of babies here, from ages of 2 weeks old up to 12 year old children. Among them are those who have Measles and Pertussis, that although may risk infection, are no longer transferred to hospitals but must stay at the barrack, one of the worst orders. Everything here is becoming more and more similar to Vught, about which they always say has a frightening children's death rate. It must be awful for everyone involved. Mrs. Landuer's mother passed away meanwhile, though it is said that her husband is feeling better.

I barely go for hospital visits anymore. Visitation hours are between 7:00 and 7:45 and I am too tired for that.

Recently I met Dr. Bale and he immediately invited me for a visit next Saturday along with Heinz.

I am glad that you stay in touch with Johan and Lena from time to time and I am curious to know how their niece is doing. Pass my regards to his wife's sympathetic parents! I am sad that I am hearing so little of the Hans', though I am pleased with news of their lives and I am in awe by their diligence. It seems that they are planning to write to me around the 30th (her 71st birthday!). In honor of that date I have a special request which is – a chunk of good soap! By the way, Ilse, the package with Tata's socks, does anyone know where it is and what is going on with it? It did not arrive, there was an error in the address and it was returned to the post office. Also, the package which had a note saying it was sent on the 10th did not arrive yet. Heinz is my loyal guest, we became good friend and we understand each other very well. He is loved anywhere!

And warm embraces for you, from Mom.

• Amersfoort - concentration camp in the center of the Nederland's

Ilse Franz and Sanne Deportation to Westerbork

Westerbork, 23.6.43

Dear friends, we could hand over our big backpacks at Daniel Willink square which were returned to us in good condition here on Monday. Afterwards we signed up and boarded the tramcar, until Muider port, the train left at 3:00, we were taken from home at 2:00. A cattle wagon, we were 28, sitting on our belongings, it was very hot with only a small crack outside. At 8:00 we arrived here, about 1,800 people and by 6:00 in the morning, we passed through all authorities, registration, identification, Y.R, Lifman, detention, redirection to a barrack, always with all the luggage, very exhausting. I am in barrack number 57, Ilse and Sanne are at number 71, much better than mine. Straight to mom, who looks thin and pale but is strong and diligent. The worst part here is the bathrooms. Disgusting! I wish I could stop everything! My bed has a straw mattress on it, Ilse sleeps on a thin mattress on one bottom bed, Sanne on the third floor, pretty nice. The food is <u>very</u> delicious, today it is lentil soup with <u>meat</u>, yesterday bread with cheese, today with two tomatoes. We will gladly receive jam, sugar, bread, butter etc. Cutting boards for bread, Franz is already missing the knife. Mom can cook, we had pudding at her place and yesterday Sanne received porridge that was left from the ill people. I would love to receive calcium for us. The barrack is huge and very full. Everyone is here, even the Rosenbaums, but we had not met yet. Hanneli and Gabby Goslar were put in an orphanage because they are motherless. This is very bad for small children. Besides that it is not so bad. For example, tonight at the barrack, I had imagined an unstoppable noise, but it was quiet for many hours. Tonight I had a deep sleep from 23:00 until 6:00, I did not hear a thing. Many ill people, which is bad. We should stay healthy. I did not contract a flea yet. Our barrack does not have tables, about 1,000 people. The hospital workers live at Ilse's barrack, a prime crowd. Heinz is very quiet, fatherly, wise, consulting, one of his letters could no longer reach us, and he asked to send his greetings to Hague.

He looks well, we met him one morning on the street and he was kind and excited. He already knew the night before we arrived. Mom is very excited, rather sad than happy. In the evenings, we are always at her place. She has a lot of authority. Phelbs is at her barrack. A postcard from *B. Had just arrived, we are very happy! Thank you! It is so nice to hear from someone. Heinz's opinion about Elz' is the same as B.'s and mine. We should not exaggerate, no one should. Dr. B is not peaceful. He has a nice apartment, it should be pleasant for the ill. Move Rosenbaum's subscription for "Nieuws uit Rotterdam" here under their name, to barrack number 67. Yesterday we visited the Kahns and Mrs. Rosyn at the hospital, they look okay but K is very sick and unaware of that. Mrs. Elsb' also looks very unwell. Yesterday football was played here. Everyone has to work here. Ilse is trying to get accepted for work with the children', if not, then some outside job. I was released from working through Albert, we are still attempting different things.

It is permitted to stay out on the street until 10 o'clock. There are so many acquaintances here that it is intangible! I brought a duvet, Elza has two green blankets, Sanne has three, one of which is on the mattress. The sofa blanket is welcome! Along with more warm blankets and later on, bed sheets and pillow covers, but not yet. There is a big deficit in the item keep. Another cooking pot, the size we would always cook potatoes in, but please do not go crazy with it. If you cannot get it, that is half the trouble. Diarrhea and coughing are a big trouble! P. De-Paris is still wearing a huge bandage due to an ear infection, he was at a Groningen hospital, besides that he has a stuffed nose and diarrhea and the little one has lung infection. We hope to pull through. We become exhausted as time goes by. The old are usually very sensitive, lots of arguing and aggression. But gratitude for good treatment is immediately appreciated.

Greetings to you, good people, and do not worry for Noorder Amstellaan st., Amsterdam anymore (the Ledermann's address in Amsterdam!).

Farewell to you free people, without freedom!

       Yours, Ilse and Franz.

The less children you have here, the better. Our only child is already too much though her behavior is excellent. Inform about the address of R. at the Merwedeplein 3. Pass my "telegraph" address to barrack number 75. A few hangers (3).

On June 20th, 1943' Ilse, Franz and Sanne edermann were taken away from their home.

- B – Barbara
- Nieuws uit Rotterdam – Rotterdam Newspaper

(A letter from grandma, to the family of the son Hans in Switzerland, was send to Paul who forwarded it).

Monday, 28.6.43

My beloved! I received your warm letter for my birthday from *Mont Pelerin as early as Wednesday. It warmed my heart and longing received an unbearable dimension. Meanwhile, your lives are moving uphill again and it is so good to know that although a lot of work was put into this, you have reached a point of relief. You must be feeling as if you were reborn as you sit together again in your nest and can get a bird-eye's view on everything that is about to happen. I am very curious to know, Dolly, if you will be accepted into university. If you find the time, along with your studies and work, maybe write to me about it.

And you, Vincent my dear, write about your new school. You must have so many friends already, even on the cable railway, on which I rode a few times at 1900 when your father was not even born yet.

Did you also take part at the beautiful daffodil celebration at Montreux? And picked the lovely flowers by yourselves? It caused me so much joy at the time! It is nice and gladdening, Hans, that you have such interesting lectures, it is a shame that I cannot participate from up closer and learn from them myself. Question is would it still get in my old head, I am afraid not. My intensive activity from 6:00 in the morning to sometimes 12 at night demands all of my energy. That is probably what is happening with you as well dear Ruth, (Ruth worked at the laundry area of the camp in Switzerland). It is good that modern machines somehow make work easier.

I received the news of the Ledermanns coming here with very mixed emotions. We are now meeting more than we ever did. They come over every evening after work, meaning between 8 and 8:30, together with Heinz. We can sit here on the stools by the table, though not alone of course, and for a moment forget where we are. Of course I am happy that I will not be alone of the 30th the day of my golden marriage celebration. Your letters, Paulien, as well as the packages that arrived in the last two weeks, made me very happy. Everything is useful and welcome. What we are lacking the most at the moment are bread and butter and maybe jam, which you are probably lacking as well. We had lately received 3 packages with 5 eggs, a cucumber, bread, tomatoes and 5 peaches from Charlotta and Lizzie. I cannot describe how fast everything disappeared in our 5 stomachs (including Heinz's). Again, Liska added black bread to the package she sent to Dr. Polack for me, how nice of her. Two days afterwards, she wrote me a nice letter.

Apparently you were worried again, I hope for nothing. Because you can never know where we really stand. Today, 16 English women went out of here without their husbands towards a closed camp in *Vittel. They, of course, thought that they would be going with their husbands, so the disappointment was great.

They also say that this week, the mixed marriages will be sent back, or more accurately, the part that is here, so tensions are high. Of course they will have to sign their "initiated" agreement to the sterilization. I had just put coffee substitute on the fire for our table. It is quite a pleasant drink although we are lacking milk, sugar and something to eat it along with it. We are pleased with the change of another drink. We must pass our letters at 5:00 so I must finish quickly. But I must still thank Paulien for her lovely letter and great paintings from which I can clearly tell how nice the birthday of Annemari was, And what lovely gifts she had received.

• Mont Pelerin - Close to Montreux Switzerland

• Vittel - Detention camp located in Northeastern France. Camp house citizens of neutral or enemy countries whom they wanted to exchange for German prisoners.

Your letter, Lynntsha, in which you write about the meeting with your friend was of much interest to us. How full of energy and initiation she is. I hope she had pleasant days at your friends'. *(It is speculated that this is about Barbara, due to being hidden is not being mentioned by her real name).

Thousands of kisses and embraces to all of you, from grandma-mom.

Kisses to Carolinetsha. How lovely it is that she is always writing by herself.

On the same page and on grandma's turn - additions from Ilse.

My dear beloved, I am fortunate to have immediately received the job that is suitable for me at the barrack of pregnant mothers and mothers with babies and small children. I do everything, starting from heating – oven treatment – washing the barrack's floors and up to laundry, baby bathing, bringing the food and helping the terrified mother as much as possible. I really need the apron I had asked to be sent and I am lacking a few blankets. Thanks to that fact that I have a good restroom, I always have food supplements and great milk. The hall manager is our friend July De-Paris.

July's mother, Mrs. Schpitz, is also living there and spoils me very much, Sanne benefits from that as well. Besides that, Bale gave me an approval for additional milk and porridge, so everything is well for me. Franz was employed at legumes sorting for half a day and can work sitting down, he hopes to join the orchestra. Sanne is employed as an assistant for the residence office. Half of her class is here, she also has friends who are seniors here and live in small houses. Last night we visited Bale, Sanne went to a circuit of young people who read Nathan the Wise and listen to lovely records.

We are receiving the *blue stamping, very promising, because of Palestine. This is the only reason why I received a job so fast otherwise I would have to work outside. The food is unbelievably delicious but requires a lot of bread. My "letter writing day" is on the 7.7 farewell! Yours the beloved Ilse, Hans and Ruth, we are hoping and thinking that you will continue to be alright.

- Blue stamping of Palestine - exchange prisoners

7.7.43 (from Franz to friends "outside" that passed it later to Paul)

Troymans, my dear,

The last letter from Ilse, This Letter from Franz. Thank you very much for your kind letter. You have no idea what the meaning of news from outside has in a place like this. Having the newspaper coming regularly now is a true comfort. It did not arrive yesterday, could you check if the subscription needs to be renewed? All three of us have now reached the phase of camp sickness, which usually happens after the first two weeks. Sanne overcame it the fastest. Ilse had a severe bout followed by unconsciousness and fever, still lying in bed and feeling very weak though the situation is already better. I am at the beginning of the bout, sometimes I have to suddenly cease my actions and I am living of solely on porridge and toast. Ilse and I are both working, she is working at the mothers' residence which satisfies her but also tires her a lot, and me sorting legumes 8 hours a day. You get used to it! There is some chance for a different, more fitting job but here it has no meaning. You get to meet and speak with so many acquaintances that you run out of subjects, after all, almost all of them are here! Please, thank the Tzillenirgers for the kind letter and to Johan Bandin. The weather is terrible. A mixed of hot sun, sand storms and heavy rains. I would avoid choosing this place for my permanent residency. Ilse and I are very grateful for the quick fulfillment of our requests that were passed by the Y.R. and for the great package with the cakes. Ilse has some time to read now that she is lying here. I on the other hand started learning Hebrew again after having stopped exactly 10 years ago. Send my regards to all the dearest and acquaintances, Yours, Franz Ledermann.

Ilse - I am already feeling better. We are saddened by Hans Goldschmidt and his mother. Franz and I see each other in the evening, there is no time for anything, on Sundays always at Bale's. Other than that no time for visitations. Thanks to *Lotta (Barbara) and Manfred (B's boyfriend) for their letter. Very pleased with everything. Is Lotta feeling better?

• Lotta (Barbara) – appeared on the Transcript, Ilse used false names to prevent Barbara detection by the Gestapo.

29.7.43

My dear, since I had just moved to Ilse's barrack – so my address is now also barrack number 71 – we have the same "writing day". This is actually the only change which is also a good one. Except working hours we are now always together. Except breakfast, we eat all the meals together and this barrack is better than the last one in all aspects. It reminds me a bit of us moving from *Machik st. to Genthiner st. . Other than that it is impossible to describe our lives here. Most importantly is that, amazingly we are healthy – even I am – at least for now, and that allows us to pass on things without hurting the mood. Although my work is tiring as time goes by, I am sitting there with very pleasant people so that is also bearable. Everyone is making an effort to make the situation easier for one another and this joint effort allows a pretty pleasant atmosphere. Added to that is the lack of external differences, the human side comes out more and it causes an understanding that is completely different from our normal lives. If you look at it, most of the people behave excellently, even in the toughest situations. It is mandatory to be healthy and hence the great importance of your deliveries. I can only repeat Ilse's words, that we are very grateful to you, Lotta's latest package excited me very much. All of it arrived in good condition, again, and helped contribute to my morale. I was very pleased with the warm words of *Manfred as well. You are all such diligent people! I am no longer in the same barrack as Zusammen, he is a very diligent person as well. Mrs. Rosyn's condition is very worrying. Recently I have seen lady Schute as well and thought how strange it is to think of our lives in the past. I am happy that Rosa (Barbara) wrote to Hans as early as last week, I am hopeful that he will hurry up and call Fritz (hastily, regarding the certificate).

The nice weather is of course a great relief but the heat sometimes weighs heavily. We enjoyed the refreshing yogurt and are very thankful for the mineral water. Overall, we are amazed by Lotta's imagination that accurately knew the things we miss, as with the candy that we miss here so much. Paul, the butter you sent arrived just in time as ours ran out, and that was by guess! Ilse is asking for small bandages to treat mosquito bites that, for some reason, are following me. I am wearing my sweatpants all day, I would wear my other pair if I had a belt. Sanne is in urgent need of a summery pair of shoes, size 35 or 36. I lost my forth towel here and cannot find another one. Do you still have something of that sort? Our sugar and pudding consumption is enormous. Thanks in advance. And on that note: we used a kilogram of salt to wash skirts, so everything ran out. With all my heart, Yours, Franz.

Ilse - many more kisses from me to the three of you. Paulien's paintings are lovely.

Sanne is always writing to Rosa (Barbara, her sister).

- Machik, Genthiner – Street Names in Berlin
- Franz use the name Mannis in the letter for Manfred Barbara's boyfriend

12.8 .43

My beloved, thank you again for the beautiful packages, the fruits are lovely. Everything came in good condition, as well as the mineral water and yesterday, the fresh beans. The Iodoform gauze is very effective against flees, send more of it. 2 knives for spreading the bread are welcome, maybe more of those should be found. The two cakes you have baked were lovely, especially the one with seasonings, we were delighted! I still have an opportunity to cook. We had not received mail in about two weeks. At this situation it is preferable to only write on postcards with the sender's full address.

By the addresses on the packages, I could tell that, god bless, all of you are healthy. I do not worry for you or for ourselves. On the contrary, the life here appeals to me, they say I look better than I did in Amsterdam. I feel less of a mental burden and can completely commit to my work, which is very tiring but also satisfying. A lot of energy is lost in the need for a woman to take care of her own household. We are all healthy. Sanne has reactions to the injection. I am happy that the Pauls' could be united. Hans wrote here to us straight from Switzerland. Ada suffered from severe postpartum depression and committed suicide, just as a friend of mine did a few years ago. I personally find that it is important to live, no matter how and where. I am happy here with my children, far more than expected. There is nothing lovelier than bathing a baby and being rewarded with a loud laughter of joy. I would work out with them as well. Although I am mainly busy with house work, eventually this is all for the sake of the children.

Mom found full satisfaction as well by treating the sick and she does wonders, everyone comes to her and she never has a quiet moment, which is exactly how she loves it. I am thinking about you with the same love you are thinking about us with and embrace you with all my power and love.

    Yours, Ilse.

23.8.43

Beloved children! The paper is terrible and so is the pen. I am carrying it without a cap with me. During the last few weeks I had only received Hans' letter with additions from Paul and could at least conclude that my last letter to you and Charlotte had reached you, as we received all the beautiful packages.

Unfortunately, Paul's last two packages arrived crushed so badly that only a few items were salvageable. It was such a shame! Of course we are longing for these fresh things. The best way to pack things is to make sure they are not moving, even if the package is being shaken. Mail in both directions will from now on arrive in larger time intervals, because each letter has to first pass censorship, therefore you are also obligated to only write on one side of the paper since otherwise it will take longer.

Meanwhile I assume that Haya is already back in Amsterdam, Lientje may have spoken with her already. If you are able to, please pass her my warmest regards. That small lady leaves a big impact everywhere she passes "a perfect person!" how rare is that these days... The Ledermanss completely adapted and Ilse always loyally brings me my share of the packages. We had and still sometimes have lovely summer weather, contrary to the days when it is hard to put up with the cold and the rain, then the work that was an acceptable habit, becomes the hardest. The day before yesterday, August 21st, Tata's 81st birthday. Is she still alive? I could almost wish she was not. Sanne is suffering from tonsillitis and has to stay in bed until her fever drops. She is always happy with Charlotta's great packages. She wore the shirt and the shoes immediately. Everything fits and is truly beautiful. There are no new events, so enough. We are thinking and talking about you every day. Constant longing. I hope you are all healthy!

Embraces, with my love, Mom.

26.8.43

My Dearest,

Today your lovely letter arrived and we were very happy about it. And now your birthday is coming up soon. You know what I wish for you. Dearest, I know you don't have it easy, I do hope that you will face all the challenges in the future with the same calm and care you have had until now. As soon as the packages arrive we were close to tears while unpacking them.

Sanne is lying sick right now in bed with inflamed glands and I with strong stomach ache but its not making us unhappy though. We do not need to tell you how thankful we are of you, I am sure you can imagine it without a lot of thought.

Please stay healthy and happy as ever, and send best wishes to our loved ones.

Yours truly, Franz

26.8.43

My beloved *Lizzy!

This now has to be my birthday letter to you. I think back to all the other birthdays we were able to celebrate together and where I was able to choose a gift for you with joy and love. Now you have become the one to worry and to send gifts.

But my heart is with you and I am thankful that you are *here, not only for you but for my sake as well.

I wish for you, with the deepest emotion that a human being can gather, happiness with your friends, happiness in your work, and love for life in all its beauty.

May everything come as a blessing to you.

Feel yourself being hugged and on the *4th we will be seeing each other again and be together.

In the package from the 5th of August, the bread had mould all over it. So please do not send this type of bread anymore, but rather some German bread or rye bread. and please don't waste all your money on us.

Sanne has caught angina 14 days ago and was very sick. It could take a little longer for her to recover, she is lying down with your headscarf. She is very happy with your gifts and will dictate me a letter to you later on. she sleeps on the third floor so I will have to climb to her bed.

Sal meanwhile has an injured hand and can hardly write. lately we see him more often and he sends his regards and love.

Grandma was sick and forgotten about your birthday in her last letter, and she send her love.

The meadow around us is in full bloom. Everyday it's shining brighter the trees, the far away rooftops the clouds and colorful displays of the sky.

We send you and your beloved ones kisses and love.

    Yours, Ilse.

- Lizzy is Barbara
- Here meaning the letters connection with the family
- 4th September Barbara's Birthday

26 Aug, 43

Sweetheart,

It will probably be around your birthday when you get this letter. Sweetheart, you know, I would rather have told you this in person with a present. It hasn't happened often, not true, that we didn't celebrate your birthday together and that's why it's a bit weird to send you a birthday kiss, instead of giving you a big peck on the cheek. And the present, or rather presents, I got them from you this year, instead of you getting presents from me! Variation is good from time to time. The things you send were beautiful! First came the shoes. Naughty! Weren't those shoes yours? I swear I remember you just got them. You can't send me things, that you need yourself, hear me! Of course I was very happy to get them and they fit me perfectly. They were marveled at here! And that cute blouse. Wonderful fabric, truly. I narrowed the sleeves a little and I only wear it when I just want to feel very pretty. The scarf idem ditto, idem ditto. Although I am wearing it in bed right now. I am sick once again since Sunday. Mononucleosis. I have a swollen, and painful gland, in combination with a headache and a severe fever. This morning at 8:30 my temperature was 38.4. Annoying, right? The doctor said it could last three weeks. I am writing in bed, as you can tell, it doesn't go that well. I am wearing the scarf, filled up with non-absorbent and regular cotton wool , I look like I have the mumps. The belt is nice too. It's of great quality. I was overjoyed with that well-known game of patience. But I don't understand that other game. Too bad, right? The packet full of candy was amazing! I was already sick when I got it and I finished it in 2 days! Oh, it's so exciting to get mail! Those shoes from Pl. were amazing (again!) They fit like a glove. It's like I have a shoe shop. Although two pair of shoes are not that much over here in W. because the shoe soles wear down quickly especially when you are an orderly. This morning we got your letter written on the 5th. getting your finger stuck can hurt pretty bad. How did Bea react? See, I knew that you and Manfred would get along just fine. Congratulations, Manfred, with "the girl of your dreams", or isn't she? Are you giving her tulips again this year? But I bet you won't be as shy this time, because there won't be as many people around now! O right, Lientje, I have to ask you for a grocery bag and a tea strainer and tell Louisje her honey cake was unforgettably good. Is she back? The weather has been good lately, she was very lucky. Uncle Heins wants to give his loving regards, lots of kisses and birthday wishes, and furthermore have a great birthday and an incredible amount of kisses from your

    Susje (Sanne)

P.S. Thank you for "Willy soffer" , I was already familiar with it, but the beauty of it strikes me again. Manfred you will get a separate letter from me, because of the "occasion", doesn't that please you?

    Bye sweethearts…

9 sep, 43

Sweetheart.

As you can tell, I am healthy again. Although I spent 12 days in bed and that was more than enough. But now it's dad, inconvenient right? And he was just so proud of himself for staying healthy. Now I am seeing the dentist regularly. The first time was just a silly cavity, but the second time (just now) it appears that yet again a nerve had to be removed. Fortunately the dentist is very kind, he understands how to do a tooth drilling, on someone who isn't fond of a procedure like that. Steffie, his 14 year old daughter sleeps next to me, which is a lot of fun. When I was sick I was looked after by a nurse, sister Wollheim, I believe she is an old acquaintance of yours. She is a sweetheart. Unfortunately, she is no longer in the barracks. I was extremely delighted with the last bulk of books. And of course I was also happy with those beautiful socks. You made them yourself? I don't think so, but they are lovely anyway. I am always in need of warm clothing. Once you wrote me something about a warm jacket. We didn't talk about it further, but if you could still get your hands on it, I would be happy to receive it. Also we ran out of hairpins. Those birthday presents you send were indescribable. We literally ran out of everything and we long for the evening mail. Will there be anything in it for us? How was your birthday? I bet it was nice. Manfred shouldn't say you are not smart, because you have proven through everything that you are.

I am in the room all by myself and I am thinking of you and of my tooth. Both hurt (how poetic, right?). After all, homesickness is just part of it. Although you were totally wrong, when you wrote that we must be sad all the time or we would like to hear something that is not sad once in a while, but actually we aren't sad at all here, just sometimes (because of a letter or something) and you don't show it to the others. Do you get it? So feel free to write something cheerful. Such wonderful gifts you gave Marga, I bet she was happy! Glad to hear Manfred and you worked things out. I understand completely when you live together you'll run into difficulties from time to time, but afterwards it will be better than before. Almost like 80 years, right? You always said I was an old auntie. So now you can't tell me that anymore, so I'm becoming one!

Did I thank Pauline already for those little French books? They are very nice, even though I don't know much of it anymore now. Now I am busy learning all those words. So Pauline, thank you. I also received your card. How was Friesland? Beautiful till the end? Because when you read this you'll be back home again. Are you in school? I realize I know so little about you. You should write me a long (illustrated) letter one day, so I know what you are up to all day. So I'll get that letter. You don't quite understand, how great it is to receive letters here. I believe Lottie* understands, because I get lovely long letters (not all too often) from her, after half an hour I know them word for word by heart. Today I got a jacket from a girl whom it didn't fit anymore. It's a fairly proper winter jacket, just what I needed, because the other one is too thin. See, I was right when I thought those shoes were yours. You showed me them once.

Sometimes we have a cat at the table, he comes to beg for food. He is small. Just like our Stip but in stripes. How do you think our little Stip is doing? We had such a great time with that animal. Do you remember how he fell down? (Of course, you will say). Sweetheart, I'll leave it at this. Say hi to all the other sweethearts and many kisses to you, enough to last you for the next two weeks

    Yours Sanne.

• Lottie is Barbara

11.9.43

My Dearest,

Unfortunately I have to write to you from my bed. My stomach ache would not be cured by any medicine, so my doctor sent me to a specialist who sent me to the hospital, where I am now. I have to wait for six days while they are running some new tests and I will have to get a special diet and lay in bed all the time, which can take from 4 to 6 weeks. Those are periods of time that you don't like to imagine in the long run.

All the same right now I have nothing better to do, since the pain is gone, resting in bed, where they take good care of me. the only good moments are the visiting hours in the evening.

I'm delighted of your wonderful packages, because right now I can eat anything besides meat, but I fear that after the six days of diagnosis this will change. But please receive my warmest thanks for all of your love and for all the packages you sent.

What you write about yourself interests us of course into every detail, you could not be elaborate enough.

I feel bitter of course, because I can't rest at the family's dining table, but maybe this will also pass.

Mother is still fabulous and I feel very incapable beside her. Please give everyone of our dearest friends and family my best regards.

      Franz

Westerbork, 7.10.1943

My dearest friend,

Today we are having a birthday party for the first time here. We have done our best despite the circumstances to make it a special day for Sanne and it seems to have worked, because when she got out of bed today to get her birthday kiss – my only present for her – she was laughing as expected from a soon to be teenage girl.

The preparations were of course all in Ilse hands, being sick i couldn't help much and its makes me worry about the future.

My deepest thanks for your wonderful packages which are helping us immensely. I would like to ask you for a favor, It is turning very cold at night, would you kindly try and get some flannel shirts? and my razor blades are running out as well.

Sanne was very happy about your Get Well Card, which was received yesterday. Thanks very much to you and Manfred.

The sausage gave us lots of good lunchtime memories – will we ever have memories like these again?

Sanne just came right now and tells me that a big package just arrived. It seems like it will be a real birthday after all.

Please give my regards to all our loved ones and friends, especially Paul and Iden, who we also thank a lot.

   With love, yours Franz

W. 20.10.1943

My dear friends,

First of all, thank you for your wonderful letter from the 5th of August, which arrived here on the 8th of October. We are thinking fond of you all in deep friendship. The knitted dress for Gaby Goslar arrived in good condition and is being word by her all the time. Everyone adores it. I myself have 24 injections behind me and, I can say without exaggerating, without any effect. My stomach aches are still the same and if I am to believe the doctors here I will have to live with them for the rest of my life, if they stay as tolerable as they are still.

It seems that this will depend on my diet, nursing and rest though the chances of that happening are pretty low.

Therefore I keep silent, more often in deep thought, as I feel more and more that I am a burden to my dear ones. But this also will pass. Heinz still remains in the hospital. Of course we visit him daily, often more than once and he is patient as ever.

Most of the time we go and visit Annemarie as well, she is in hospital due to a small operation, but she is happy as she can be.

But of course there are nice things to report as well. We once again thank you, Lientje and Paul for the wonderful packages we receive. Especially the Swedish bread was a treat, way better than the rye bread. Every diversion of the local bread would be very refreshing. The honey was also wonderful.

The flowers and the golden vase arrived and were met with excitement in the whole barrack. The two birthdays passed in silence, Sanne met with friends for coffee and cake.

Right now I am on office duty.

        Feel loved from yours – Franz

PS. Could you send us some Esbit or Burning Material? We are in need of those.

Transcript of handwritten Postcard from Ilse, sent before boarding the train to Auschwitz with husband Franz and daughter Sanne.

16.11.43

My loved ones, we are together with Kathe on our first longer journey in a long time. Grandmother is sitting extra.

It's all right for the time being. We're with 43, that could have been worse. Everyone has given us a tremendous amount of food. It's difficult for Mom and Heinz…

Don't be sorrowful for us, we have good hopes and it would only hurt us if you were sad. We want to see each other again.

My *Barbel child, take care. Your last parcels still delicious. We've got porridge with us. Also dad's bathrobe, the wool and everything sent to Granny.

Friendly people here. All still without certificate. We're going, by darlings. All the love, all the best. Bye.

Your Ilse

(murdered in Auschwitz on 19.11.43)

• Barbara, Ilse daughter, stayed in Amsterdam with falsified certificates supplied with the help of the Dutch resistance and her boyfriend Manfred

Transcript of the last postcard sent by Ilse Ledermann

(Karte von Ilse – handgeschrieben...)

16. 11. 43

Meine Geliebten, Wir sitten mit Käthe zusammen auf unserer ersten grösseren Reise seit langer Zeit. Die Grossmutter sitzt extra. Es geht vorläufig. Wir sind 45, dat valt mee. Alle haben uns entsetzlich viel Lebensmittel mitgegeben. Für Mutti u. Heinz ist es arg. Grämt Euch nicht um uns, wir haben guten Mut und mir wenn Ihr traurig wärt, würde uns das quälen. Wir wollen uns wiedersehen.

Mein Bärbelkind, hou je hazi. Dat wenschen we nu allemaal. De groeten an Mammi, Jullie laatste pakketten nog heerlijk. De pa hebben we mee. Ook Papas badjas, de wol en alles nam Ome stuuren. Nette Leute hier. Alle noch ohne Zertifikat. Wir fahren, dag schatten. Het liefste, beste, Daag

Jullie Ilse

(am 19. 11. 43 in Auschwitz ermordet)

The Ledermann Family After the war

Franz Ilse and **Sanne Ledermann** died at **Auschwitz** 19 November 1943.

Ellen Citroen died at **Bergen Belsen** 6 January 1945.

Tata and **Lala** died 5 February 1943 in Auschwitz (Pauline Schonlicht and Sophie Neumann).

Paul Lientje and **Paulien** survived the war in the Netherlands.

Hans and **Ruth** Citroen survived the war in Switzerland.

References

- Yad Vashem Museum Archive
- Barbara Ledermann interview 1990
- Diary of Anne Frank
- Memories of Anne Frank - Hanneli Goslar / Alison Leslie Gold
- Anne Frank the Biography - Melissa Muller
- Anne Frank Silent Witnesses - Ronald Wilfred Jansen
- Wikipedia
- Geni.com Website

Printed in Poland
by Amazon Fulfillment
Poland Sp. z o.o., Wrocław